Happy Thanksgiving

Coloring Book for Toddlers

Blue Wave Press

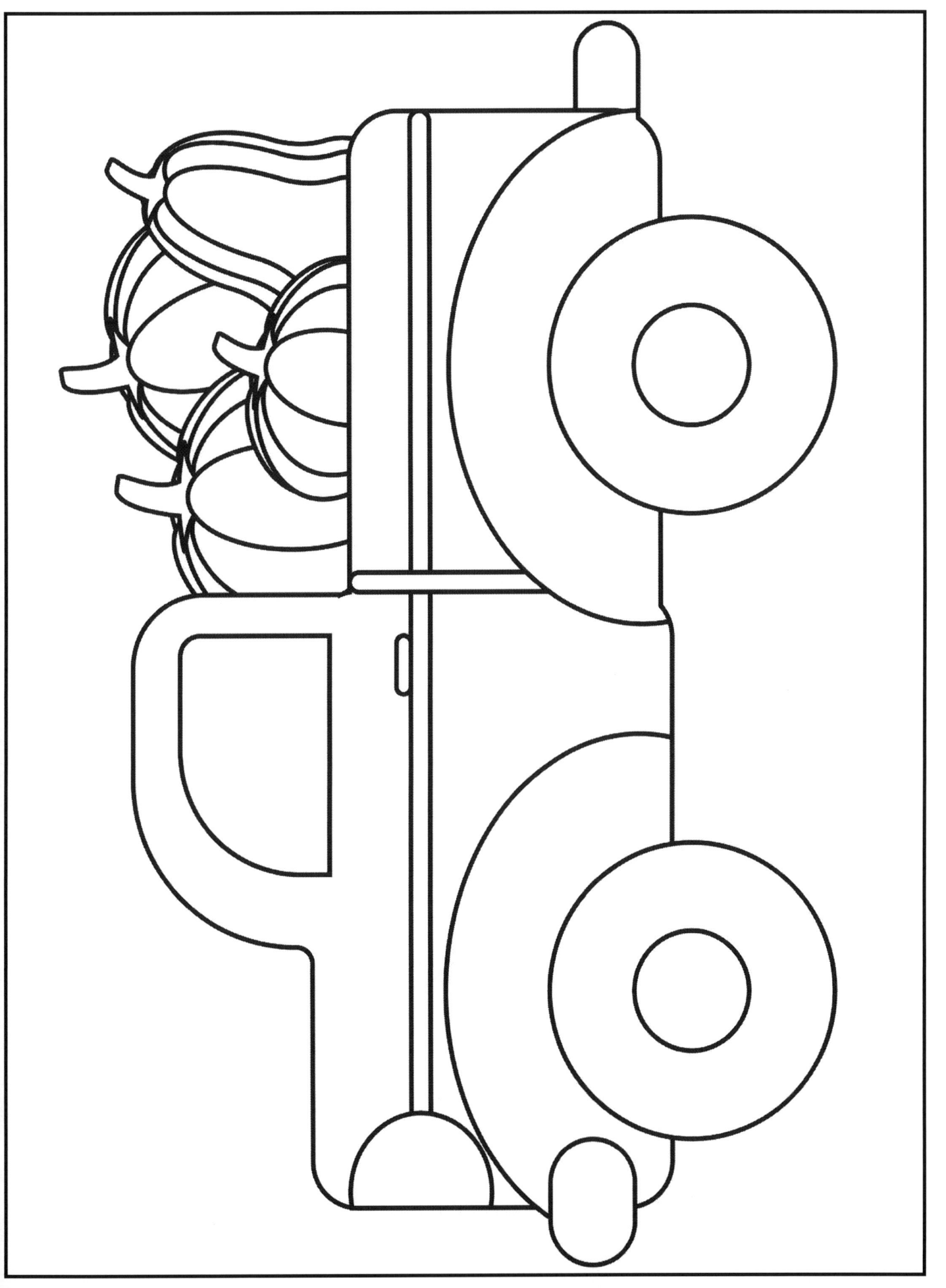

HAPPY

THANKSGIVING

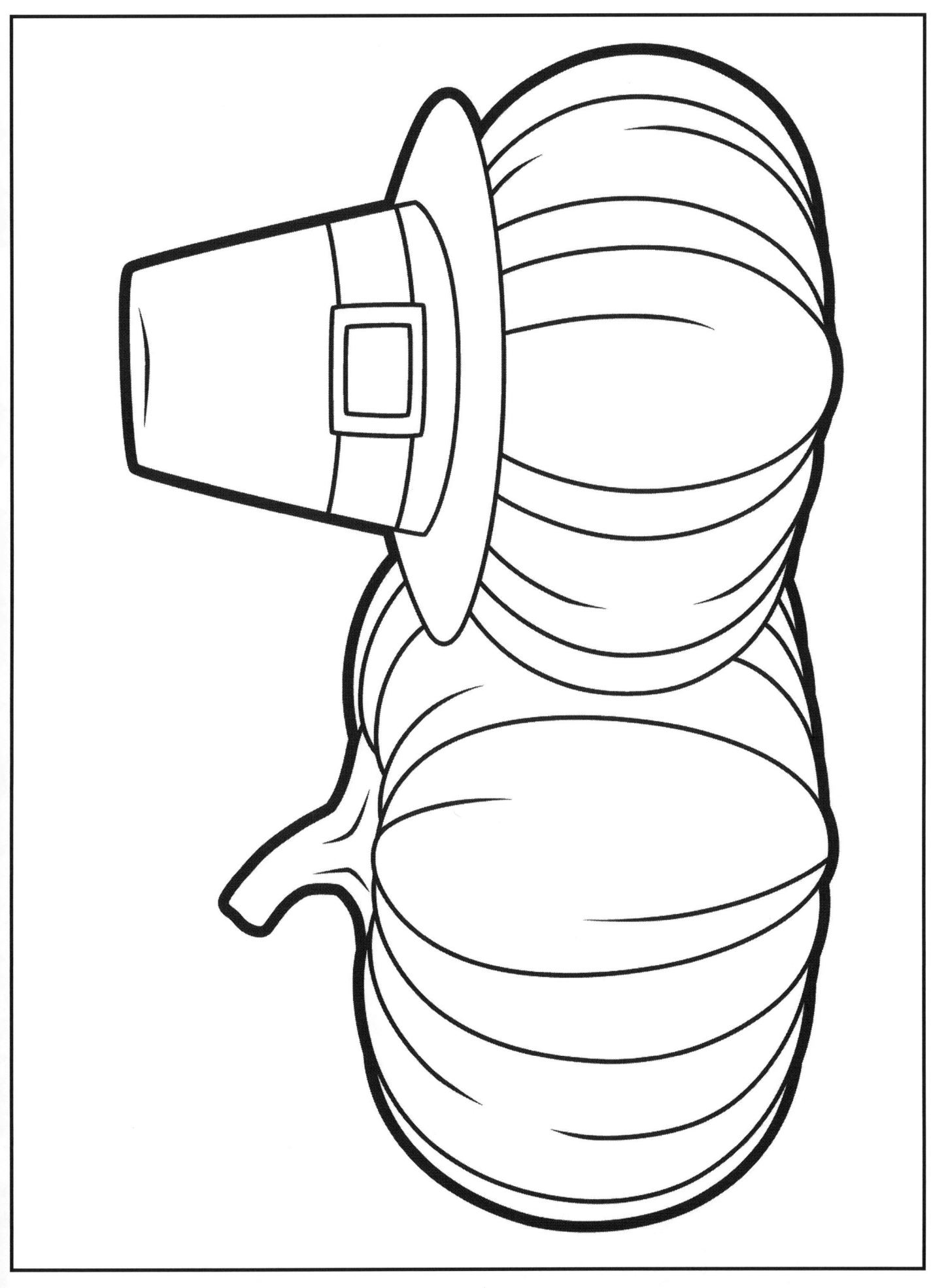

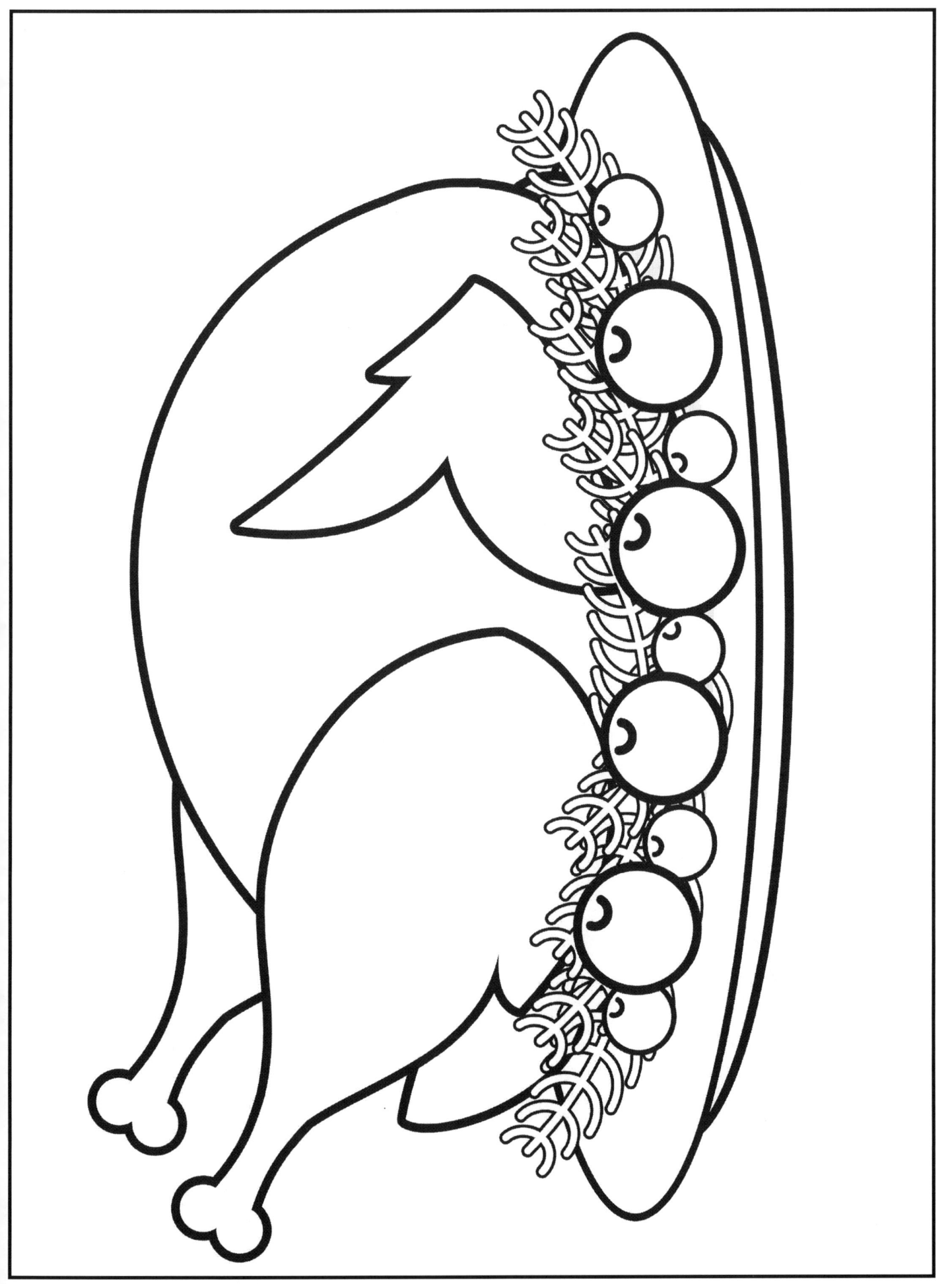

Copyright © 2019 by Blue Wave Press
All rights reserved.
First edition: 2019

Be sure to look for more of our fun and educational coloring and activity books for kids!

Made in United States
Troutdale, OR
10/18/2024